Quilts Say It Best

GATHER·FRIENDS·LIKE·FLOWERS

EILEEN WESTFALL

That Patchwork Place

Quilts Say It Best

©1997 by Eileen Westfall

That Patchwork Place, Inc., PO Box 118

Bothell, WA 98041-0118 USA

Printed in Hong Kong

02 01 00 99 98 97   6 5 4 3 2 1

Dedication

To my husband, John, with great love, in honor of our twenty-fifth wedding anniversary.

"Polly Put the Kettle On" is dedicated to the memory of Polly Klaas.

Credits

Editor-in-Chief	Kerry I. Hoffman
Technical Editor	Janet White
Managing Editor	Judy Petry
Copy Editor	Tina Cook
Proofreader	Melissa Riesland
Design Director	Cheryl Stevenson
Text and Cover Designer	Sandy Wing
Production Assistant	Claudia L'Heureux
Technical Illustrator	Laurel Strand
Illustration Assistants	Carolyn Kraft, Bruce Stout
Pencil Illustrator	Barb Tourtillotte

Library of Congress Cataloging-in-Publication Data

Westfall, Eileen.
    Quilts say it best / Eileen Westfall.
       p. cm.
    ISBN 1-56477-179-2
    1. Patchwork—Patterns. 2. Quilting—Patterns. 3. Proverbs in art. 4. Appliqué—Patterns. 5. Embroidery—Patterns. I. Title.
TT835.W486   1997   96-34442
746.46'041—dc20   CIP

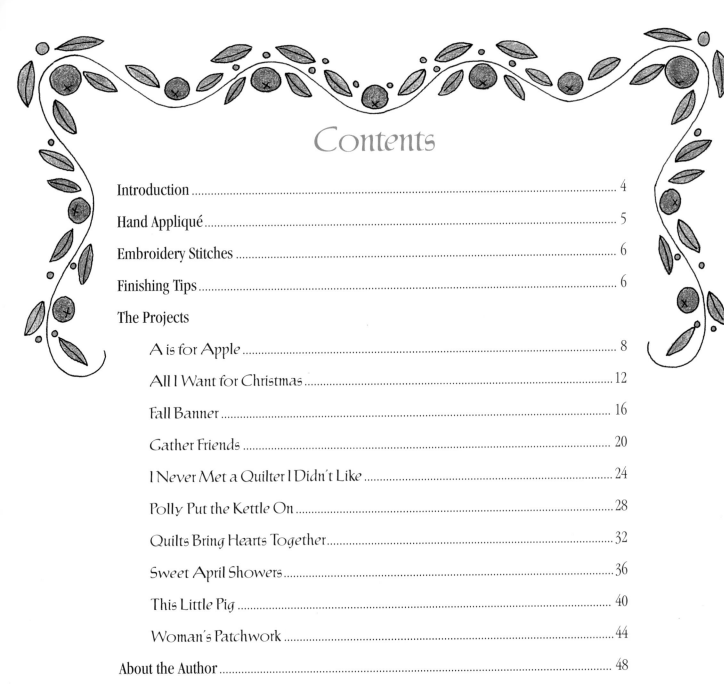

Contents

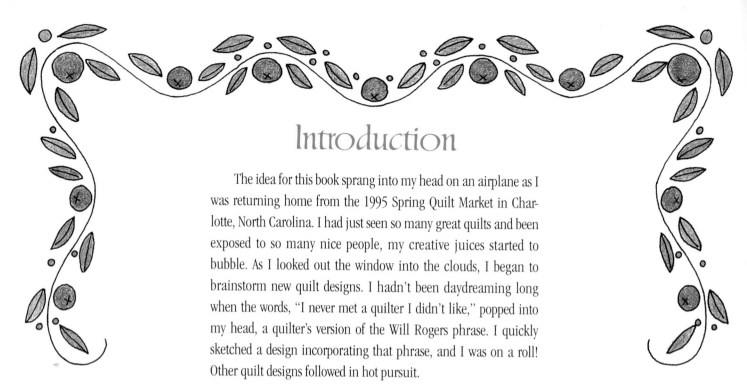

Introduction

The idea for this book sprang into my head on an airplane as I was returning home from the 1995 Spring Quilt Market in Charlotte, North Carolina. I had just seen so many great quilts and been exposed to so many nice people, my creative juices started to bubble. As I looked out the window into the clouds, I began to brainstorm new quilt designs. I hadn't been daydreaming long when the words, "I never met a quilter I didn't like," popped into my head, a quilter's version of the Will Rogers phrase. I quickly sketched a design incorporating that phrase, and I was on a roll! Other quilt designs followed in hot pursuit.

I have been sewing all my life and have always loved putting words on whatever I made. *Quilts Say It Best* is a collection of quilt designs that combine words or sayings with patchwork, appliqué, and embroidery.

All the projects in this book include complete directions and a cutting guide, which gives yardage amounts. Most cotton fabric is 44" to 45" wide, and the yardage amounts are based on 42"-wide fabric to allow for shrinkage. Full-size templates for each project can be found at the back of the book. All the projects in this book can be quilted as desired, by hand or by machine. A few quilting motifs are provided.

I enjoyed designing these fun message quilts, and I hope you enjoy making them.

Hand Appliqué

There are several methods of hand appliqué that give good results. Use the method you prefer, or follow these easy steps.

1. For each appliqué piece, make a paper template. Trace, then cut the shape from the appropriate fabric, adding ¼"-wide seam allowances.

2. Center the template on the wrong side of the fabric shape and fold the seam allowance smoothly over the template edges. Baste completely around the fabric shape, sewing through paper and fabric. Clip sharp inside curves almost to the fold.

3. Using a gluestick, spread glue on the paper template and carefully place the fabric shape on the right side of the background fabric in the spot desired. Press with a warm iron to secure.

4. Appliqué the shape to the background fabric, using small stitches that catch only 1 or 2 threads at the edge of the appliqué piece.

5. Remove the basting. Cut a small slit in the background behind the appliqué piece, and remove the paper using tweezers.

Embroidery Stitches

The four embroidery stitches shown below are the only ones you need for the projects in this book. Use three strands of embroidery floss for words and most figures, one strand for fine details.

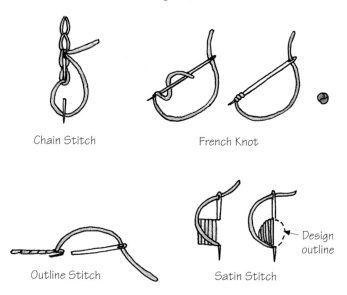

Chain Stitch

French Knot

Outline Stitch

Satin Stitch

Design outline

Finishing Tips

Basting

When your quilt top is complete, layer it with batting and backing. Baste the layers together, beginning in the center of the quilt top and using long running stitches. First, stitch in horizontal rows about 6" apart; then stitch in vertical rows. Do not remove the basting until the entire quilt top has been quilted.

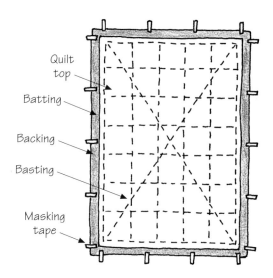

Quilt top

Batting

Backing

Basting

Masking tape

Quilting

Use care when marking the quilt top in preparation for quilting—it is important that your quilting guides be accurate. Outline quilting and other straight quilting lines do not need to be marked. Instead, use ¼"-wide quilter's tape and quilt along its edge. For some projects in this book, quilting-motif patterns are included. For others, you may want to create your own motif.

Binding

Cut enough 2½"-wide straight-grain or bias strips to go around the perimeter of the quilt plus 8".

1. Sew the strips end to end to make one long piece of binding. Press the seams open.

2. Trim one end at a 45° angle; then turn under ¼" and press.

3. Fold the strip in half lengthwise with wrong sides together; then press.

4. Starting on one side, stitch the binding to the quilt. Keep the raw edges even with the quilt top edge and use a ¼"-wide seam allowance. End the stitching ¼" from the corner of the quilt and backstitch. Clip the thread.

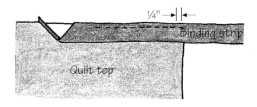

5. Rotate the quilt 90° so you will be stitching down the next edge. Fold the binding up, away from the quilt.

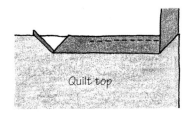

6. Fold the binding back down onto itself, parallel to the edge of the quilt. Begin stitching at the edge, backstitching to secure.

7. Repeat on the remaining edges and corners of the quilt. When you reach the beginning of the binding, trim away any excess binding at a 45° angle. Tuck the end of the binding into the fold and finish the seam, overlapping the beginning stitches by about 1".

8. Fold the binding over the raw edges of the quilt to the back and blindstitch in place, covering the machine stitching with the binding. A miter will form at each corner. Blindstitch the mitered corners in place.

A is for Apple

Finished Size: 33" x 27"

Materials and Cutting

Use the templates on pages 49–51.

Fabric (44" wide)	Yardage	No. of Pieces	Dimensions
Reds	⅜	2	6¼" x 6¼" ⊠
		4	Template 1
		2	1½" x 21½"
		2	1½" x 25"
		2	1½" x 29½"
		2	1½" x 33½"
		1 each	Templates 9, 10, 12 (page 56)
Browns	¼	1	6¼" x 6¼" ⊠
		2	Template 3
Blues	½	1	6¼" x 6¼" ⊠
		8	1½" x 7½"
		8	1½" x 11½"

Fabric (44" wide)	Yardage	No. of Pieces	Dimensions
White	½	4	4½" x 4½" ✂
		8	1½" x 7½"
		8	1½" x 11½"
		2	1½" x 23½"
		2	1½" x 31½"
		2	Template 6
		1 each	Templates 8, 8r, 11, 13 (page 56)
Medium yellow	⅛	2 each	Templates 4, 7
Light yellow	¼	2	3½" x 5½" ✂
		2	5½" x 6½" ✂
Green	Scrap	4	Template 2
Dark red	⅛	2	Template 5

Backing & binding   1⅛

31" x 37" piece of batting

Embroidery floss: black, brown, golden brown, and green

⊠   Cut twice diagonally.

✂   Cut larger than indicated; then trim to correct size after completing appliqué and embroidery.

Directions

1. Appliqué and embroider the apples, apple slices, and pie slices to the background pieces. (Refer to "Embroidery Stitches" on page 6.)

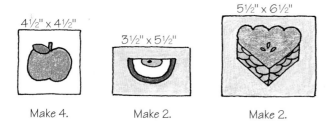

4½" x 4½"

Make 4.

3½" x 5½"

Make 2.

5½" x 6½"

Make 2.

2. Sew the blue and white strips together as shown to make strip sets.

Make 4 units, 7½" long.

Make 4 units, 11½" long.

3. Assemble the Flag blocks, using the apple squares and the strip sets.

Make 4.

4. Sew the brown, red, and blue triangles together as shown to make squares.

Make 4.

5. Sew pieces 8–13 together to make the A block.

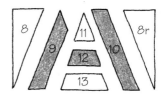

10

6. Arrange the blocks as shown below and sew them together.

7. For the inner border, sew the 1½" x 21½" red strips to the sides of the quilt top; then add the 1½" x 25" strips to the top and bottom. For the middle border, sew the 1½" x 23½" white strips to the sides; then add the 1½" x 31½" strips to the top and bottom. For the outer border, sew the 1½" x 29½" red strips to the sides; then add the 1½" x 33½" strips to the top and bottom.

8. Embroider the words, apples, and leaves on the white border.

9. Layer, baste, and quilt as desired. Bind and label your quilt.

All I Want for Christmas

Finished Size: 32" x 24"

Materials and Cutting

Use the templates on pages 52–54.

Fabric (44" wide)	Yardage	No. of Pieces	Dimensions
Dark reds	1/3	16	1⅞" x 1⅞" ◱
		1	1" x 3¼"
		1 & 1r	Template 1
		5	Template 2
		4 & 4r of each	Templates 5, 6
Light reds	1/8	8	1½" x 1½"
		2	1½" x 6½"
		4	Template 7
		8	Template 9
Gold	1/8	8	1½" x 1½"
Creams	1/4	1	6½" x 6½" ✂
		8	Template 8
White	1/3	16	1⅞" x 1⅞" ◱
		4	2¼" x 2¼" ⊠
		4	3" x 5½" ✂
		2	3" x 6½" ✂
		4	3" x 8" ✂
		2	2½" x 20½"
		1	Template 3

Fabric (44" wide)	Yardage	No. of Pieces	Dimensions
Green-and-red print	1/4	1	3¼" x 4½"
		1	1" x 4½"
Light greens	1/8	4	2¼" x 2¼" ⊠
		4	Template 7
		8	Template 10
Medium green	1/4	2	1½" x 20½"
		2	1½" x 12½"
		2	1½" x 22½"
		2	2½" x 2½"
Dark greens		8	1⅞" x 1⅞" ◱
		24	Template 4
Holly print	1/4	2	3" x 19½"
		2	3" x 32½"

Backing & binding 1¾

26" x 34" piece of batting

Embroidery floss: red, pink, and green

◱ Cut once diagonally.

⊠ Cut twice diagonally.

✂ Cut larger than indicated; then trim to correct size after completing appliqué and embroidery.

Directions

1. Sew the red and white triangles, and the light red and gold squares together as shown to make four-patch units.

Make 8.

2. Sew the red, light green, dark green, and white triangles together to make four-patch units.

 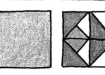

Make 8.

3. Arrange the four-patch units and the 2½" medium green squares and sew them together.

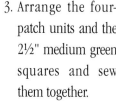

Make 2.

4. Appliqué the gift box (3¼" x 4½" green-and-red piece), lid (1" x 4½" green-and-red piece), ribbon (dark red 1" x 3¼" piece), bow, and tag to the 6½" cream block. Embroider the tag as desired. (Refer to "Embroidery Stitches" on page 6.)

5. Embroider the words on the 2½" x 20½" white strips.

$ALL \cdot I \cdot WANT \cdot FOR \cdot CHRISTMAS$

$IS \cdot A \cdot PATCHWORK \cdot QUILT$

6. Sew together pieces 7 and 8; then sew together pieces 9 and 10 to make pieced units.

Make 4.

Make 4.

7. Appliqué and embroider the holly and ribbons to the white border pieces.

3" x 6½"

Make 2.

3" x 8"

Make 2.   Make 2.

3" x 5½"

Make 2.   Make 2.

8. Sew the pieced units and the appliquéd border pieces together as shown to make the inner border strips.

9. Join the patchwork blocks, 1½" x 20½" medium green strips, Gift Box block, and word strips. Sew the 1½" x 12½" medium green strips to the sides of the quilt top; then add the remaining medium green strips to the top and bottom. Repeat with the appliquéd border strips.

10. Sew the 3" x 19½" holly-print strips to the sides of the quilt top, then add the remaining holly-print strips to the top and bottom. Add the holly and bows to complete the appliqué at the corners of the inner borders.

11. Layer, baste, and quilt as desired. Bind and label your quilt.

Fall Banner

Finished Size: 28" x 19"

Materials and Cutting

Use the templates on pages 55–56.

Fabric (44" wide)	Yardage	No. of Pieces	Dimensions
Browns	¼	5	1⅞" x 1⅞" ◱
		1	1½" x 1½"
		2	1½" x 3½"
		2	1½" x 4½"
		2	1½" x 5½"
		1 each	Templates 9, 10, 12
		2	Template 5
		1	Template 7
White	½	5	1⅞" x 1⅞" ◱
		2	1½" x 1½"
		2	1½" x 2½"
		4	1½" x 3½"
		1	1½" x 4½"
		2	3½" x 3½"
		1	5½" x 20½" ✂
		1 each	Templates 8, 8r, 11, 13
Medium green	¼	2	1½" x 11½"
		1	1½" x 20½"
		2	1½" x 22½"

Fabric (44" wide)	Yardage	No. of Pieces	Dimensions
Dark green	Scrap	1 & 1r	Template 2
Leaf print	½	2	3½" x 13½"
		2	3½" x 28½"
Orange	Scrap	2	Template 3
		1	Template 6
Dark brown	Scrap	2 each	Templates 3, 4
Dark red	Scrap	2	Template 1

Backing & binding   1

21" x 30" piece of batting

Embroidery floss: dark brown, orange, and green

◱ Cut once diagonally.

✂ Cut larger than indicated; then trim to correct size after completing appliqué and embroidery.

Directions

1. Assemble the Letter blocks as shown.

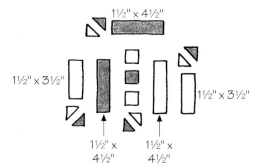

1½" x 4½"

1½" x 3½"

1½" x 3½"

1½" x
4½"

1½" x
4½"

Make 1.

Make 1.

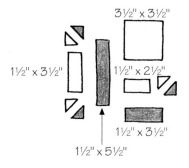

3½" x 3½"

1½" x 3½"

1½" x 2½"

1½" x 3½"

1½" x 5½"

Make 2.

2. Appliqué and embroider the leaves, apples, pie, and nuts on the 5½" x 20½" white background strip. (Refer to "Embroidery Stitches" on page 6.)

3. Sew together the Letter blocks, pie strip, and sashing.

4. Sew the 3½" x 13½" leaf-print strips to the sides of the quilt top. Add the remaining leaf-print strips to the top and bottom.

5. Layer, baste, and quilt as desired. Bind and label your quilt.

1½" x 22½"

1½" x 20½"

1½" x 11½"

1½" x 22½"

Gather Friends

Finished Size: 22" x 22"

Materials and Cutting

Use the templates on pages 57–59.

Fabric (44" wide)		Yardage	No. of Pieces	Dimensions	Fabric (44" wide)		Yardage	No. of Pieces	Dimensions
☐	White	½	1	14½" x 14½" ✂	■	Purple	⅛	1 & 1r	Template 1
								1	Template 2
☐	Orange	¼	16	2½" x 2½"					
☐	Medium green	⅓	40	1½" x 1½"	☐	Dark green	¼	1	1" x 13"
									(Cut on bias.)
☐	Yellow	⅛	24	1½" x 1½"		Backing & binding		1	
☐	Pink	⅛	16	1½" x 1½"		24" x 24" piece of batting			
☐	Lavender	⅜	4	2½" x 18½"		Embroidery floss: green, dark purple, light purple, orange, and light orange			

✂ Cut larger than indicated; then trim to correct size after completing appliqué and embroidery.

Directions

1. To make the stem circle, appliqué the 1" x 13" dark green strip to the 14½" white square; use the placement diagram on page 57. Appliqué and/or embroider the buds, leaves, and words as desired.

2. Sew together the pink, medium green, and orange squares to make four-patch units.

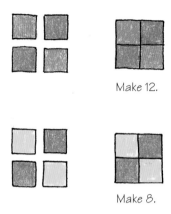

Make 12.

Make 8.

3. Sew the four-patch units and the 2½" orange squares together as shown. Sew the strips to the top and bottom of the appliqué center block.

Side Borders
Make 2.

Top and Bottom Borders
Make 2.

4. To make side borders, sew the remaining pink-and-green four-patch units to 2 purple strips.

2½" x 18½"

Side Borders
Make 2.

5. Sew the side borders to the quilt top; then add the remaining purple strips to the top and bottom.

6. Layer, baste, and quilt as desired. Bind and label your quilt.

I Never Met a Quilter I Didn't Like

Finished Size: 19" x 31"

Materials and Cutting

Use the templates on pages 60–61.

Fabric (44" wide)	Yardage	No. of Pieces	Dimensions	Fabric (44" wide)	Yardage	No. of Pieces	Dimensions
Golds	¼	4	1½" x 1½"	Greens	⅛	4	1½" x 1½"
		3	4¼" x 4¼" ⊠			4	1½" x 9½"
		2	1½" x 9½"			4	Template 1
Yellow		2	Template 4	Rose	¼	8	1½" x 1½"
Dark purples	¼	3	4¼" x 4¼" ⊠	Light pink	Scrap	1	4¼" x 4¼" ⊠
		2	1½" x 1½"				
		8	Template 2	Medium pinks	¼	4	1½" x 9½"
						2 each	Templates 3, 5
Light purples	⅜	2	1½" x 9½"	Floral print	¼	2	2½" x 19½"
		1	4¼" x 4¼" ⊠			2	2½" x 27½"
White	¼	3	3½" x 15½" ✄	Backing & binding	1		
		8	3½" x 3½"	21" x 33" piece of batting			
				Embroidery floss: dark purple			

⊠   Cut twice diagonally.

✄   Cut larger than indicated; then trim to correct size after completing appliqué and embroidery.

Directions

1. Embroider the words; then appliqué the flowers, stars, and hearts to the 3½" x 15½" white strips.

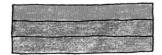

2. Sew together the 1½" x 9½" strips as shown to make strip sets.

Make 2.

Make 2.

3. Assemble the nine-patch centers; then arrange them with the squares and triangles to make the Star blocks.

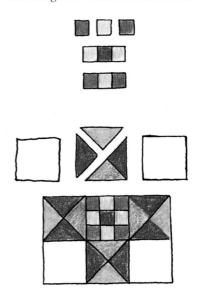

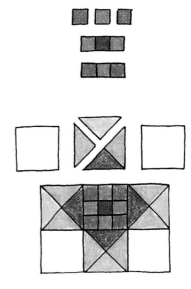

26

4. Sew together the Star blocks, strip sets, and appliquéd strips.

5. Sew the 2½" x 27½" floral strips to the sides of the quilt top; then add the remaining floral strips to the top and bottom.

6. Layer, baste, and quilt as desired. Bind and label your quilt.

Polly Put the Kettle On

Finished Size: 24" x 25"

Materials and Cutting

Use the templates on pages 62–65.

Fabric (44" wide)	Yardage	No. of Pieces	Dimensions
White	½	1	10½" x 11½" ✂
		4	4½" x 4½" ✂
		2 each	Template 6, 7, 9
Light blues	½	2	4½" x 11½" ✂
		2	4½" x 4½" ✂
		1	4½" x 10½" ✂
		1 each	Templates 1, 2, 4, 12, 12r
Brown	¼	1	2½" x 4½" ✂
		2 each	Templates 8, 11
Dark blue	⅛	4	1½" x 1½"
		2	Template 10
Yellows	¼	2	1½" x 18½"
		2	1½" x 19½"
		1 each	Templates 3, 5

Fabric (44" wide)	Yardage	No. of Pieces	Dimensions
Floral print	⅓	2	2½" x 21½"
		2	2½" x 24½"
		12	Template 12
Green	¼	6	1" x 6" (Cut on bias.)
		24	Template 13
		12	Template 15
Gray	Scrap	2	1" x 6" (Cut on bias.)*
Backing	⅞		
Binding	¼		

26" x 27" piece of batting

Embroidery floss: dark blue, dark green, brown

✂ Cut larger than indicated; then trim to correct size after completing appliqué and embroidery.

*Kettle handles can be embroidered if you prefer.

Directions

1. Appliqué the kettle and the 1" x 6" gray strips to the 10½" x 11½" white background in numerical order. Appliqué and/or embroider the flower motif on the kettle. (Refer to "Embroidery Stitches" on page 6.)

2. To make stems, fold the 1" x 6" green strips in half lengthwise, wrong sides together. Stitch the long raw edges together, using a ¼"-wide seam allowance. Fold the seam allowance under, and appliqué the stems to the background strips as shown. Appliqué and/or embroider the buds, leaves, and words on the blue and brown background blocks.

Wrong sides together

4½" x 11½"

4½" x 10½"

4½" x 11½"

2½" x 4½"

3. Appliqué and embroider the tea bags, cups, and tea jars to the blue and white background blocks.

Make 1 and
1 reversed.

Make 2.

Make 1 and
1 reversed.

4. Arrange the appliquéd and embroidered blocks as shown and sew them together. Sew the 1½" x 19½" yellow strips to the sides of the quilt top. To make the top and bottom borders, sew a 1½" blue square to each end of each 1½" x 18½" yellow strip. Add the top and bottom borders to the quilt top.
5. Sew the 2½" x 21½" floral strips to the sides of the quilt top; then add the remaining floral strips to the top and bottom.
6. Layer, baste, and quilt as desired. Bind and label your quilt.

Quilts Bring Hearts Together

Finished Size: 24" x 27"

Materials and Cutting

Use the templates on pages 66–67.

Fabric (44" wide)	Yardage	No. of Pieces	Dimensions	Fabric (44" wide)	Yardage	No. of Pieces	Dimensions
White	½	1	16½" x 19½" ✂	Rose	¼	4	1½" x 8½"
						4	1½" x 11½"
Medium green	¼	4	2⅞" x 2⅞" ◻			8	3½" x 3½"
		2	1" x 3"				
			(Cut on bias.)	Medium pink	¼	8	3½" x 3½"
		2	1" x 2½"			4	2⅞" x 2⅞" ◻
			(Cut on bias.)			38	1½" x 1½"
		4	1" x 3½"				
			(Cut on bias.)	Light pink	¼	16	2⅞" x 2⅞" ◻
Dark green	¼	16	2⅞" x 2⅞" ◻	Backing & binding	1¼		
Dark blue	¼	8	3½" x 3½"	26" x 29" piece of batting			
		8	2⅞" x 2⅞" ◻	Embroidery floss: dark green			
		38	1½" x 1½"				
Light blue	⅛	8	3½" x 3½"				

◻ Cut once diagonally.

✂ Cut larger than indicated; then trim to correct size after completing appliqué and embroidery.

Directions

1. Sew together 3½" squares to make four-patch units. Using Template 1 on page 66, cut 1 heart from each four-patch unit.

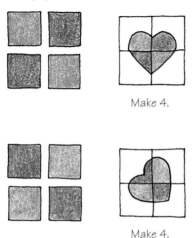

Make 4.

Make 4.

2. To make stems, fold the green bias strips in half lengthwise, wrong sides together. Stitch the long raw edges together, using a ¼"-wide seam allowance. Fold the seam allowances under and appliqué to the 16½" x 19½" white background piece.

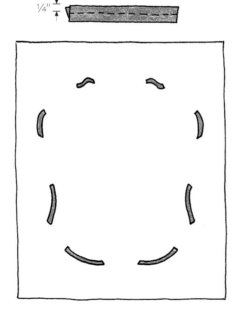

3. Appliqué the hearts and embroider the leaves, tendrils, and words on the background. (Refer to "Embroidery Stitches" on page 6.)

4. Sew triangles together as shown to make the Diamond and Pinwheel blocks.

Diamond Block
Make 4.

Pinwheel Block
Make 8.

5. Sew the 1½" pink and blue squares together to make pieced strips. Sew the pieced strips and 1½" x 11½" rose pieces together; then add the Pinwheel and Diamond blocks to make border strips.

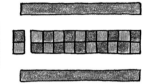

Side Borders
Make 2.

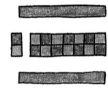

Top and Bottom Borders
Make 2.

6. Sew the side borders to the quilt top; then add the top and bottom borders.
7. Layer, baste, and quilt as desired. Bind and label your quilt.

Sweet April Showers

Finished Size: 22" x 20"

Materials and Cutting

Use the templates on pages 68–69.

Fabric (44" wide)		Yardage	No. of Pieces	Dimensions	Fabric (44" wide)		Yardage	No. of Pieces	Dimensions
	Light blue	1/8	2	2½" x 12½"		Light pink	1/8	4	2½" x 2½" ✂
			2	2½" x 14½" ✂		Dark pink	1/8	4	Template 7
			2	Template 9				10	Template 8
	Dark Blue	1/4	1	Template 1		Maroon	1/8	2	Template 2
	White	5/8	1	10½" x 14½" ✂		Floral print	G	2	2½" x 16½"
	Medium green	1/8	1 & 1r	Template 3				2	2½" x 20½"
			1 & 1r	Template 4					
	Dark green	1/8	1	2½" x 14½"					
	Brown	1/8	1	1" x 11½" (Cut on bias.)					
	Yellows	1/8	1 & 1r	Template 5					
			3 & 3r	Template 6					

Backing & binding   1¼

22" x 24" piece of batting

Embroidery floss: yellow, green, dark green, pink, maroon, and blue

✂ Cut larger than indicated; then trim to correct size after completing appliqué and embroidery.

Directions

1. Sew the 2½" x 14½" dark green strip to the bottom of the 10½" x 14½" white piece to make the center block.

2. To make the umbrella handle, fold the brown bias strip in half lengthwise, wrong sides together. Stitch the long raw edges together, using a ¼"-wide seam allowance. Position the umbrella handle on the background, folding under the ends and the seam allowance. Appliqué in place.

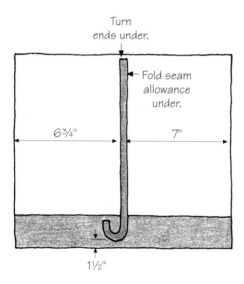

Turn ends under.

Fold seam allowance under.

6¾"   7"

1½"

3. Appliqué the shapes to the center block in numerical order. Embroider the small flowers and raindrops. (Refer to "Embroidery Stitches" on page 6.)

4. Appliqué the hearts to the light pink squares, and then embroider the words on the 2½" x 14½" white strips as shown. Sew a light pink heart square to each end of each embroidered strip.

 SWEET·APRIL·SHOWERS

 BRING·MAY·FLOWERS

5. Sew the 2½" x 12½" blue strips to the sides of the center block; then add the embroidered strips with the Heart blocks to the top and bottom.

6. Sew the 2½" x 16½" floral strips to the sides of the quilt top; then add the remaining floral strips to the top and bottom.

7. Layer, baste, and quilt as desired. Bind and label your quilt.

THIS·LITTLE·PIG
WENT·TO
MARKET
THIS·LITTLE·PIG
STAYED·HOME

This Little Pig

Finished Size: 33" x 33"

Materials and Cutting

Use the templates on pages 70–72.

Fabric (44" wide)	Yardage	No. of Pieces	Dimensions	Fabric (44" wide)	Yardage	No. of Pieces	Dimensions
Light pink	⅓	16	3⅞" x 3⅞" �«cut once diagonally»	Light turquoise	½	1	11½" x 11½" ✂
		4	Template 3			8	2½" x 2½"
Dark pinks	⅛	8	2⅞" x 2⅞" �«cut once diagonally»	Dark turquoises	⅝	2	4⅞" x 4⅞" �«cut once diagonally»
		8	1½" x 1½"			16	3⅞" x 3⅞" �«cut once diagonally»
Light green	⅛	8	2½" x 2½"			2	2⅞" x 2⅞" �«cut once diagonally»
Medium greens	¼	2	4⅞" x 4⅞" �«cut once diagonally»	White	1	4	8½" x 11½" ✂
		2	2⅞" x 2⅞" �«cut once diagonally»			20	2⅞" x 2⅞" �«cut once diagonally»
		8	1½" x 1½"			4	3½" x 3½"
		4	Template 1				
Dark green	Scrap	4	Template 2				

Backing & binding   1⅜

35" x 35" piece of batting

Embroidery floss: brown, dark green, lime green, and dark pink

�«cut once diagonally» Cut once diagonally.

✂ Cut larger than indicated; then trim to correct size after completing appliqué and embroidery.

Directions

1. Embroider the words, apples, berries, and leaves on the 11½" light turquoise square. (Refer to "Embroidery Stitches" on page 6.)

2. Appliqué the pigs to the 8½" x 11½" white rectangles; then embroider the details.

3. Sew the triangles and squares together as shown to make the Corn and Beans blocks.

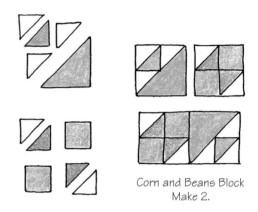

Corn and Beans Block
Make 2.

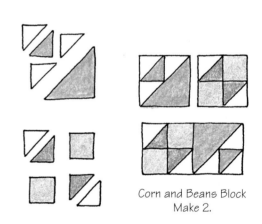

Corn and Beans Block
Make 2.

4. Sew the Corn and Beans blocks, the Pig blocks, and the center block together as shown.

5. Appliqué the apples to the 3½" white squares and embroider the details. Sew the light pink and dark turquoise triangles together to make half-square triangles. Sew the 1½" dark pink and medium green squares together to make four-patches.

Make 4.   Make 32.   Make 4.

6. Sew the four-patches, half-square triangles, and Apple blocks together as shown to make borders.

Side Borders
Make 2.

Top and Bottom Borders
Make 2.

7. Sew the side borders to the quilt top; then add the top and bottom borders.
8. Layer, baste, and quilt as desired. Label and bind your quilt.

Woman's Patchwork

Finished Size: 24" x 22"

Materials and Cutting

Use the templates on pages 73–75.

Fabric (44" wide)	Yardage	No. of Pieces	Dimensions	Fabric (44" wide)	Yardage	No. of Pieces	Dimensions
White	½	1	11½" x 12½" ✂	Dark pink	⅛	16	1½" x 1½"
		24	1½" x 1½"			4	1⅞" x 1⅞" ◿
		16	1⅞" x 1⅞" ◿			2	Template 10
		4	2½" x 2½" ✂	Yellow	⅛	8	1½" x 2½"
		1	3½" x 12½" ✂			8	1½" x 4½"
		1	4½" x 12½" ✂			2	Template 11
		1	Template 9	Green	⅛	4	1½" x 1½"
Light blue	¼	2	1½" x 12½"	Gray	¼	1 each	Templates 1, 2, 4
		4	1½" x 20½"	Orange	Scrap	2	Template 11
		2	1½" x 24½"				
Medium blue	¼	8	1⅞" x 1⅞" ◿				
		1 each	Templates 5, 7				
		4	Template 12				
Dark blue	⅛	4	1½" x 1½"				
Light pink	¼	16	1½" x 1½"				
		1 each	Templates 3, 6, 8				
		4	Template 10				

Backing & binding   1

24" x 26" piece of batting

Embroidery floss: dark blue, green, and black

◿ Cut in half once diagonally.

✂ Cut larger than indicated; then trim to correct size after completing appliqué and embroidery.

Directions

1. Appliqué and embroider the vines, flowers, and hearts to the 11½" x 12½" white piece. (Refer to "Embroidery Stitches" on page 6.) Add the sewing-machine pieces, appliquéing them to the background in numerical order.

2. Embroider the words on the white background rectangles.

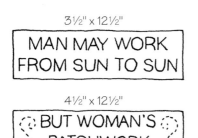

3. Sew the triangles and squares together as shown to make the corner blocks.

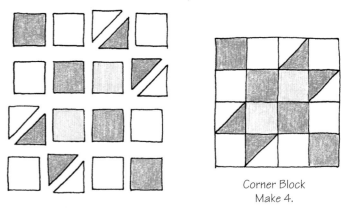

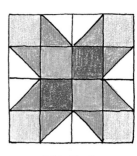

Corner Block
Make 4.

4. Sew the triangles and squares together as shown to make the side blocks.

Side Block
Make 2.

5. Appliqué the hearts to the 2½" white squares. Sew the 1½" x 2½" yellow strips to the sides of the squares. Add the 1½" x 4½" strips to the top and bottom.

Make 4.

6. Arrange the blocks and sashing strips as shown; then sew them together. Add the border strips.

7. Layer, baste, and quilt as desired. Label and bind your quilt.

MAN MAY WORK
FROM SUN TO SUN

BUT WOMAN'S
PATCHWORK
IS NEVER DONE!

About the Author

A lover of quilts since she was a child and a designer for more than twenty years, Eileen Westfall is the author of numerous magazine articles and eight books on quilting, including *Basic Beauties: Easy Quilts for Beginners* (That Patchwork Place). She currently lives with her husband, John, their son Damian, and a cocker spaniel named Josey in a quilt-filled house in Walnut Creek, California.

A is for Apple
Templates

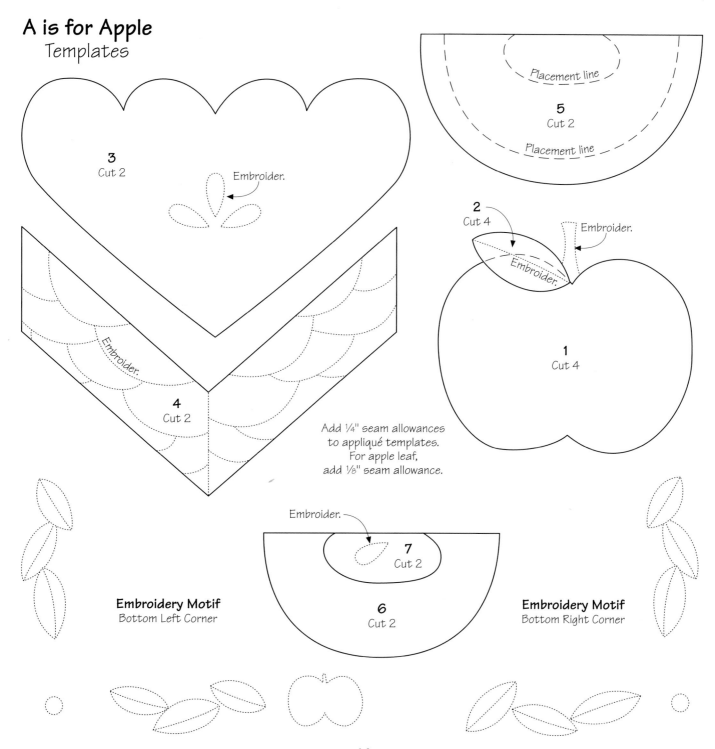

3
Cut 2

Embroider.

5
Cut 2

Placement line

Placement line

2
Cut 4

Embroider.

Embroider.

1
Cut 4

Embroider.

4
Cut 2

Add ¼" seam allowances
to appliqué templates.
For apple leaf,
add ⅛" seam allowance.

Embroider.

7
Cut 2

6
Cut 2

Embroidery Motif
Bottom Left Corner

Embroidery Motif
Bottom Right Corner

A is for Apple
Templates and
Lettering Guides

Embroidery Motif
Top Left Corner

Embroidery Motif
Top Right Corner

JUICE • CIDER
• PANCAKES •
JELLY

BETTY • BRE
AD • CRISP •
• BUTTER •
FRITTERS

A LA MODE •
SAUCE •
STRUDEL •
TURNOVER

DUMPLINGS
• CAKE •
PAN DOWDY

All I Want for Christmas
Templates

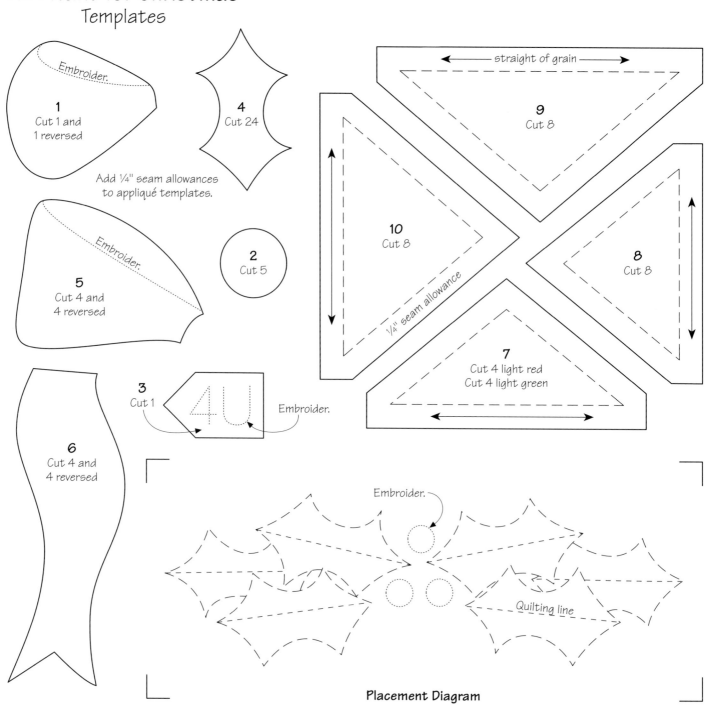

Embroider.

1
Cut 1 and
1 reversed

4
Cut 24

Add ¼" seam allowances
to appliqué templates.

Embroider.

5
Cut 4 and
4 reversed

2
Cut 5

6
Cut 4 and
4 reversed

3
Cut 1

4U

Embroider.

straight of grain

9
Cut 8

10
Cut 8

8
Cut 8

¼" seam allowance

7
Cut 4 light red
Cut 4 light green

Embroider.

Quilting line

Placement Diagram

52

A L L · I · W A N

T · F O R · C H R

I S T M A S

IS·A·PAT
CHWORK
·QUILT

Fall Banner
Templates

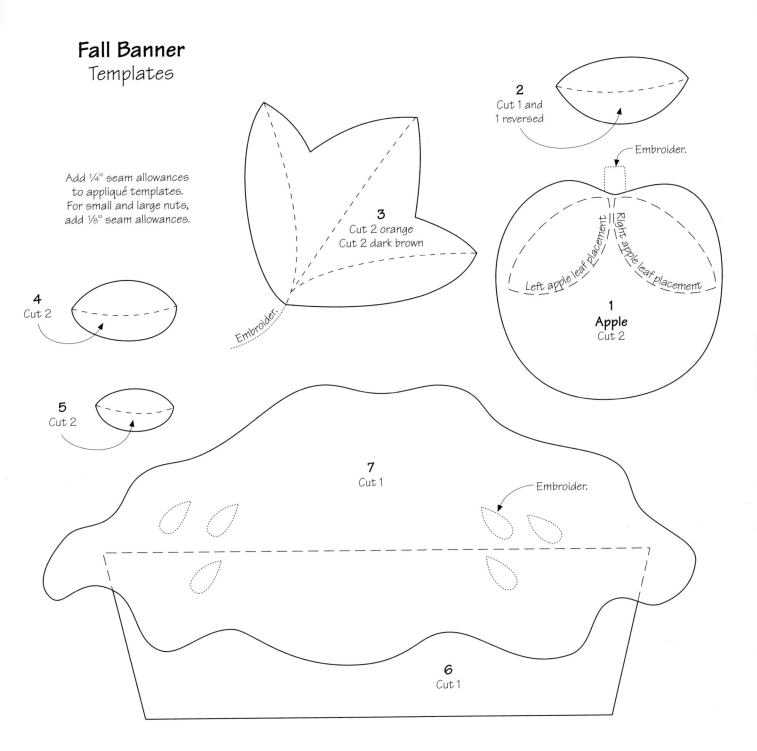

Add ¼" seam allowances to appliqué templates. For small and large nuts, add ⅛" seam allowances.

2
Cut 1 and 1 reversed

Embroider.

Left apple leaf placement   Right apple leaf placement

1
Apple
Cut 2

3
Cut 2 orange
Cut 2 dark brown

Embroider.

4
Cut 2

5
Cut 2

7
Cut 1

Embroider.

6
Cut 1

Fall Banner
Templates

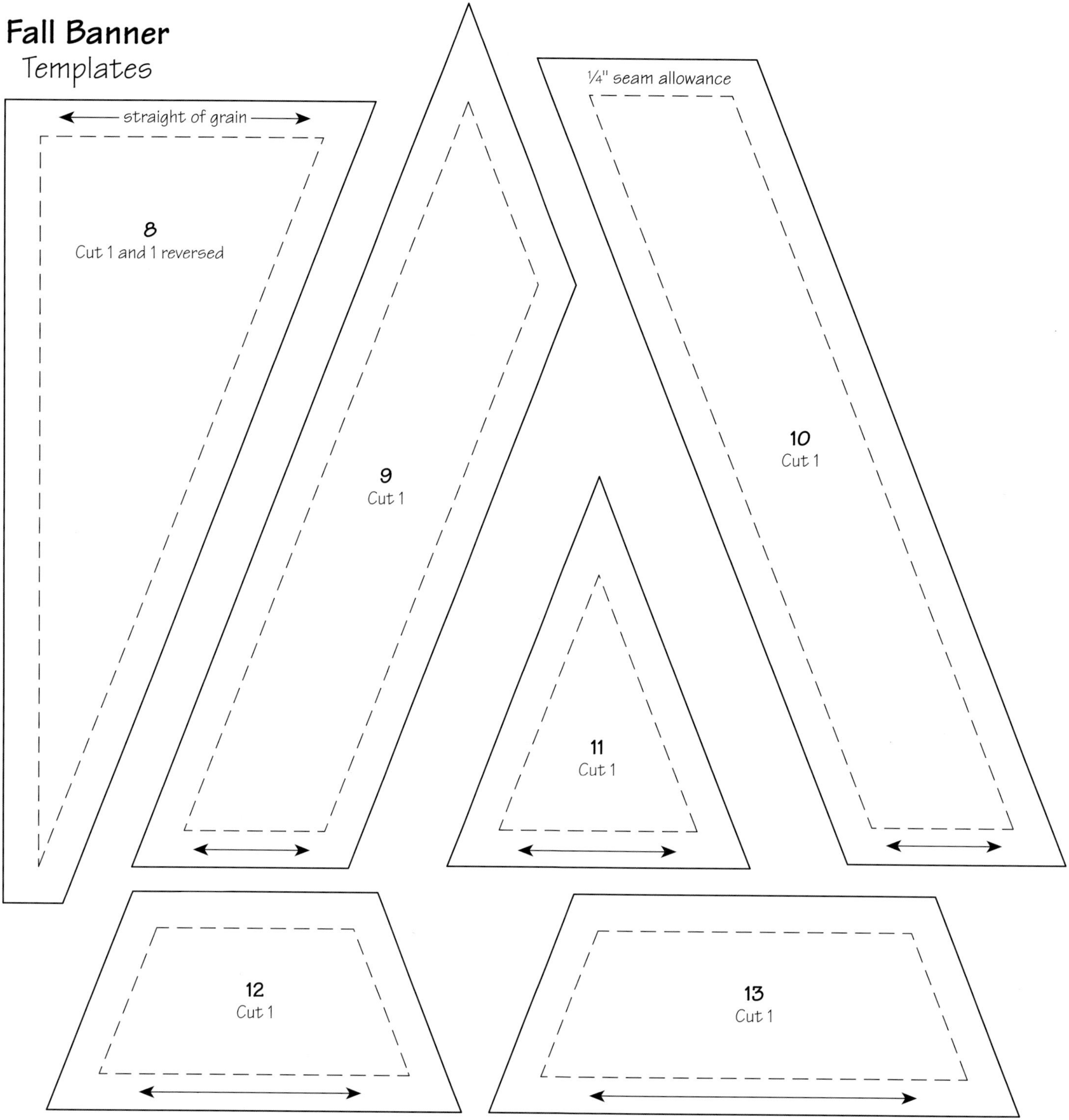

straight of grain

8
Cut 1 and 1 reversed

9
Cut 1

¼" seam allowance

10
Cut 1

11
Cut 1

12
Cut 1

13
Cut 1

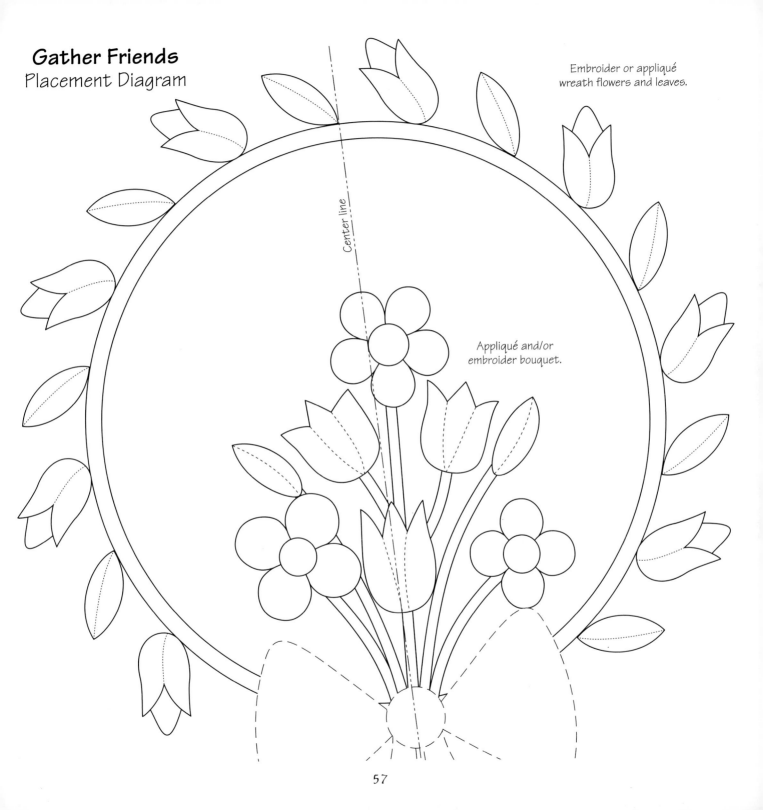

Gather Friends
Placement Diagram

Embroider or appliqué
wreath flowers and leaves.

Center line

Appliqué and/or
embroider bouquet.

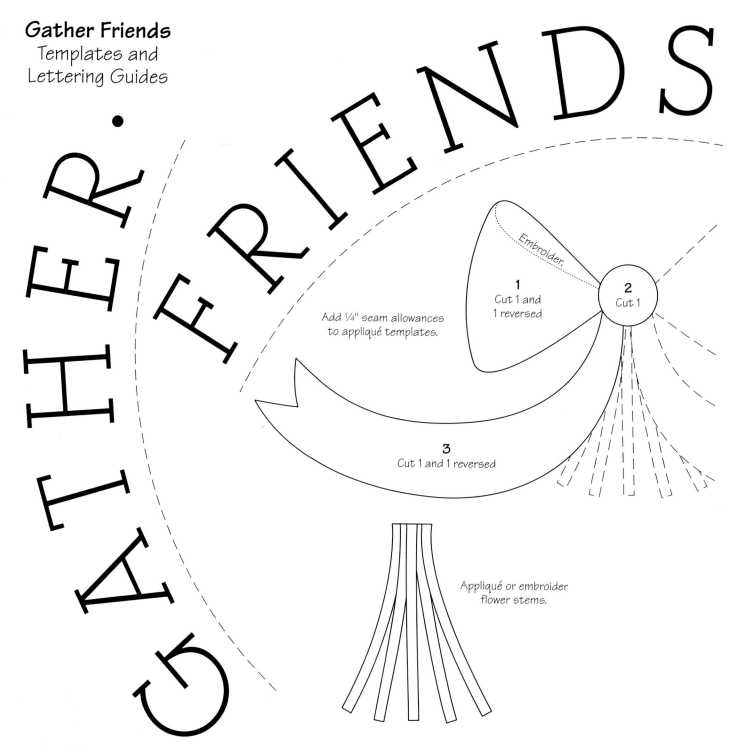

Gather Friends
Templates and
Lettering Guides

GATHER · FRIENDS

Embroider.

1
Cut 1 and
1 reversed

2
Cut 1

Add ¼" seam allowances
to appliqué templates.

3
Cut 1 and 1 reversed

Appliqué or embroider
flower stems.

Gather Friends
Templates and
Lettering Guides

FLOWERS

·LIKE·

Embroider or appliqué
corner bud and vine motifs.

**I Never Met a Quilter
I Didn't Like**
Templates and
Lettering Guides

Add ¼" seam allowances
to appliqué templates.

4
Cut 2

5
Cut 2

2
Cut 8

3
Cut 2

1
Cut 4

I NEVER
MET
A

QUILTER I DIDN'T LIKE!

Polly Put the Kettle On
Templates

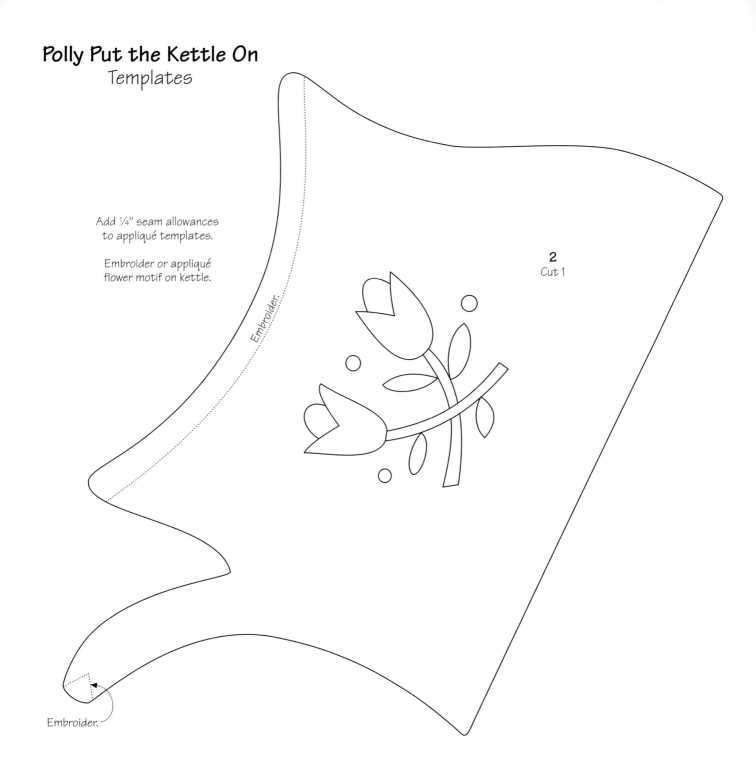

Add ¼" seam allowances
to appliqué templates.

Embroider or appliqué
flower motif on kettle.

Embroider.

2
Cut 1

Embroider.

Polly Put the Kettle On
Templates

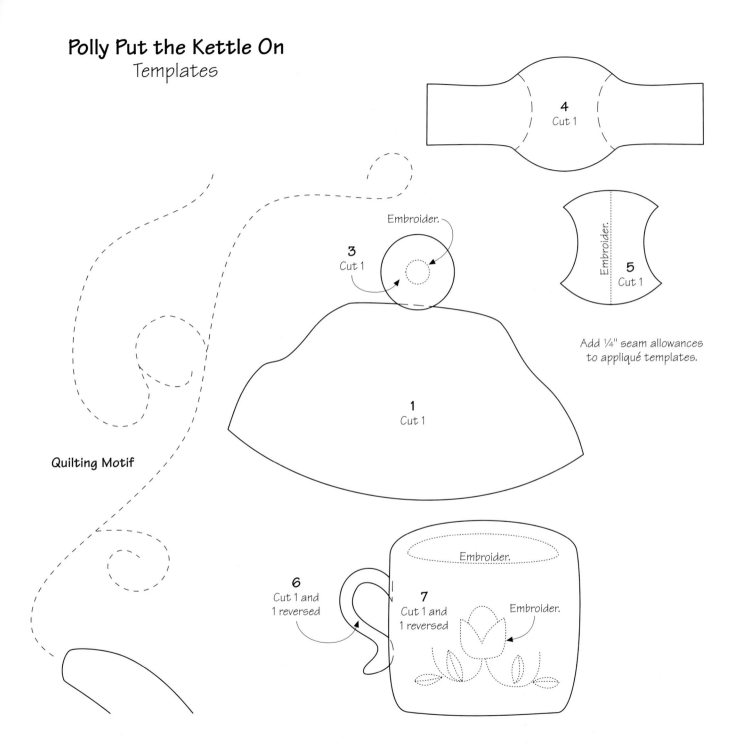

4
Cut 1

Embroider.

3
Cut 1

Embroider.

5
Cut 1

Add ¼" seam allowances
to appliqué templates.

1
Cut 1

Quilting Motif

Embroider.

6
Cut 1 and
1 reversed

7
Cut 1 and
1 reversed

Embroider.

Polly Put the Kettle On
Templates and Lettering Guides

Add ¼" seam allowances to appliqué templates.

14
Cut 8

15
Cut 8

Embroider.

13
Cut 8

Embroider or appliqué leaves and buds.

12
Cut 2

11
Cut 1 and
1 reversed

Embroider.

Oolong
Tea

Earl
Grey

10
Cut 2

Embroider.

8
Cut 2

9
Cut 2

POLLY
PUT THE

KETTLE

TEA

ON

WE'LL ALL

HAVE

Quilts Bring Hearts Together
Templates and Lettering Guides

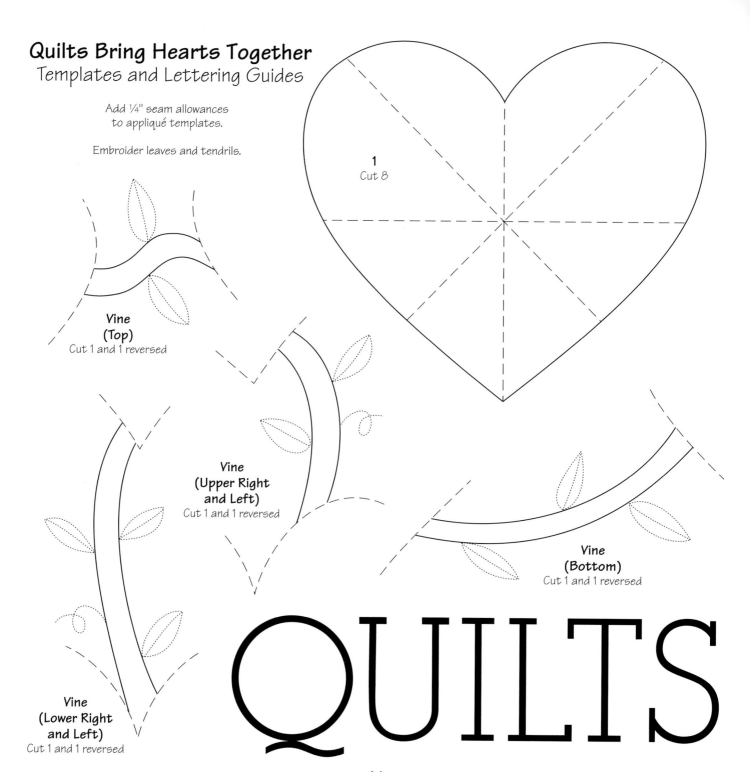

Add ¼" seam allowances
to appliqué templates.

Embroider leaves and tendrils.

1
Cut 8

**Vine
(Top)**
Cut 1 and 1 reversed

**Vine
(Upper Right
and Left)**
Cut 1 and 1 reversed

**Vine
(Bottom)**
Cut 1 and 1 reversed

**Vine
(Lower Right
and Left)**
Cut 1 and 1 reversed

QUILTS

BRING

HEARTS

TOGE

THER

Sweet April Showers
Templates

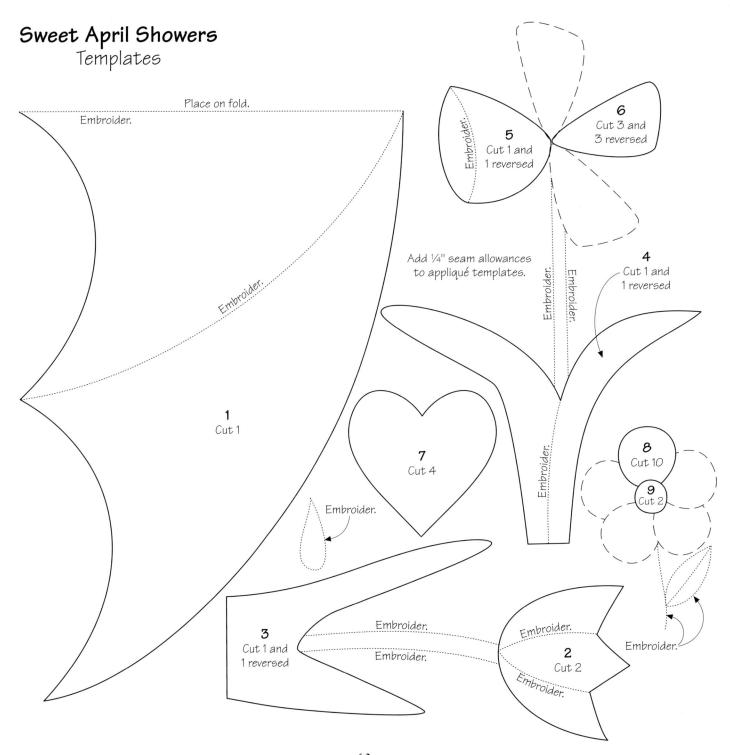

Place on fold.

Embroider.

Embroider.

Embroider.

5
Cut 1 and
1 reversed

6
Cut 3 and
3 reversed

Add ¼" seam allowances
to appliqué templates.

Embroider.

Embroider.

4
Cut 1 and
1 reversed

1
Cut 1

7
Cut 4

Embroider.

Embroider.

8
Cut 10

9
Cut 2

3
Cut 1 and
1 reversed

Embroider.

Embroider.

Embroider.

2
Cut 2

Embroider.

Embroider.

SWEET·APRIL
·SHOWERS
BRING·MAY·
FLOWERS

This Little Pig
Templates

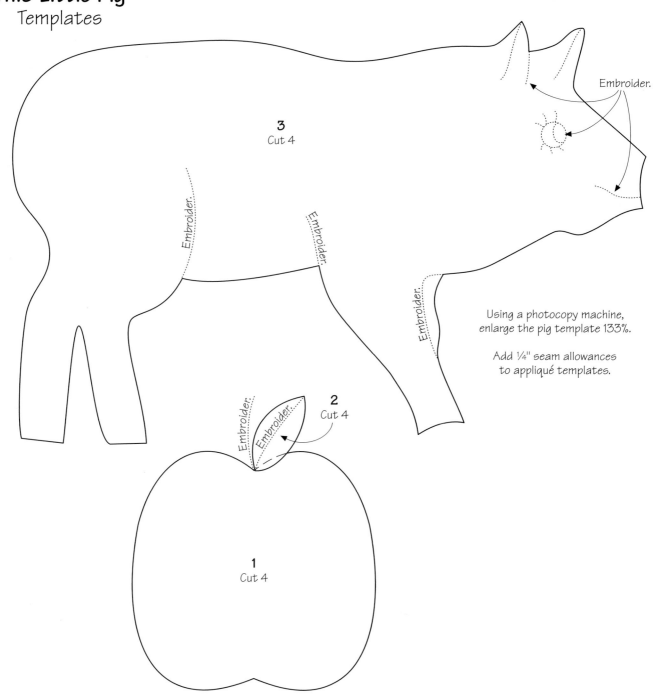

3
Cut 4

Embroider.

Embroider.

Embroider.

Embroider.

Embroider.

Embroider.

2
Cut 4

1
Cut 4

Using a photocopy machine,
enlarge the pig template 133%.

Add ¼" seam allowances
to appliqué templates.

This Little Pig
Templates and Lettering Guides

Embroidery Details for Pig

Note: Pig details are actual size; there is no need to enlarge as for pig template.

Tail
Trace onto pig.
Embroider with a satin stitch.
Use 3 strands of embroidery floss.

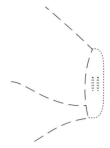

Nose
Trace onto pig.
Embroider with a backstitch.
Use 3 strands of embroidery floss.

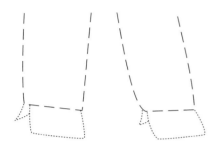

Back Hooves
Trace onto pig.
Embroider, outlining with a backstitch
and filling in with a satin stitch.
Use 3 strands of embroidery floss.

Front Hoof
Trace onto pig.
Embroider, outlining with a backstitch
and filling in with a satin stitch.
Use 3 strands of embroidery floss.

THIS·LITTLE ·PIG

Embroider.

WENT·TO

MARKET

STAYED·

HOME

Woman's Patchwork
Templates

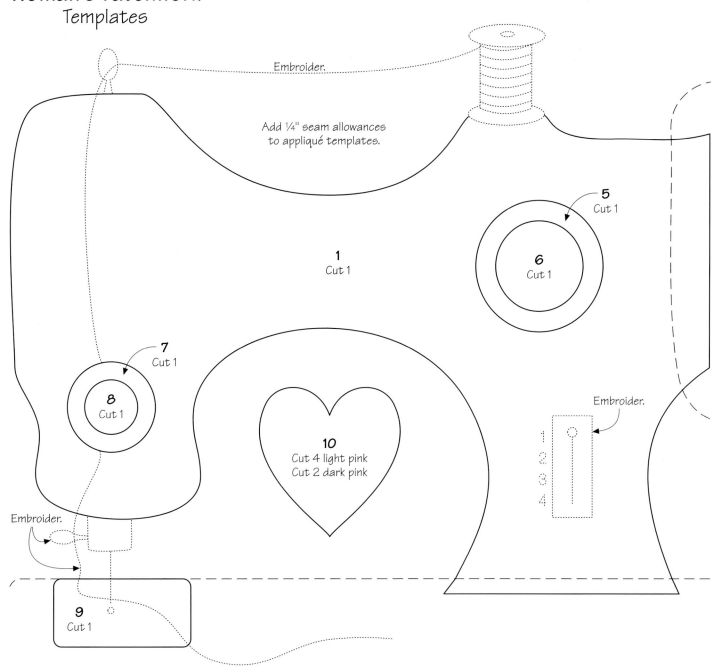

Embroider.

Add ¼" seam allowances
to appliqué templates.

1
Cut 1

5
Cut 1

6
Cut 1

7
Cut 1

8
Cut 1

10
Cut 4 light pink
Cut 2 dark pink

Embroider.

1
2
3
4

Embroider.

9
Cut 1

MAN MAY

WORK

FROM

SUN

TO

2
Cut 1

Add ¼" seam allowances
to appliqué templates.

Embroider.

11

12
Cut 4

Cut 2 yellow
Cut 2 orange

BUT WOMAN'S PATCHWORK

IS NEVER DONE!

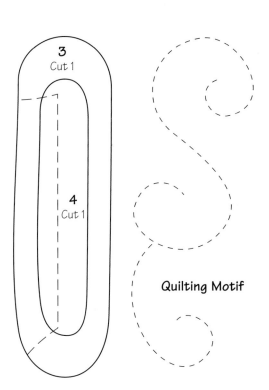

Add ¼" seam allowances
to appliqué templates.

3
Cut 1

4
Cut 1

Quilting Motif

Gift Tag

1. Photocopy the gift tag onto stiff paper, such as card stock.
2. Fold the tag in half and trim off the dashed line completely with a paper cutter or craft knife.
3. Embellish the tag with colored pencils (markers may bleed).

Quilt Label

1. Transfer a photocopy of the quilt label onto fabric using a transfer medium, or trace the label with a permanent marker.
2. Trim on the dashed lines.
3. Use embroidery or a permanent marker to fill in the quilt name, your name, the year, city, state, and recipient if the quilt is a gift.
4. Turn under the edges and stitch the label to the back of the quilt.

Publications and Products

Many titles are available at your local quilt shop.
For more information, write for a free color catalog
to That Patchwork Place, Inc., PO Box 118, Bothell,
WA 98041-0118 USA.

☎ U.S. and Canada, call **1-800-426-3126** for the
name and location of the quilt shop nearest you.
Int'l: 1-206-483-3313   **Fax:** 1-206-486-7596
E-mail: info@patchwork.com
Web: www.patchwork.com   2.97